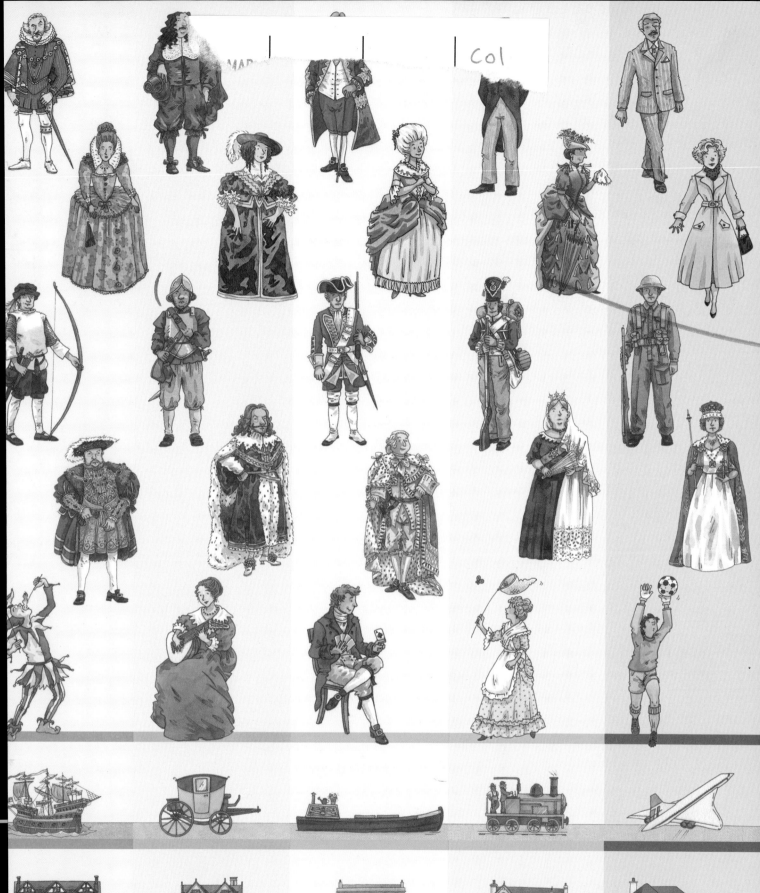

TUDOR
1485–1603

STUART
1603–1714

MODERN TIMES
1901–NOW

children's HISTORY of
KENT

Written by
Caroline Plaisted

DISCOVER MORE OF YOUR TOWN
HOMETOWN WORLD

| 500 BC | 400 BC | 300 BC | 200 BC | 100 BC | AD | AD 100 | AD 200 | AD 300 | AD 400 | AD 500 | AD 600 | AD 7 |

How well do you know your county?

Have you ever wondered what it would have been like living in Kent when the Romans invaded? What about sheltering in secret underground tunnels during the war? This book will uncover the important and exciting things that happened in this wonderful county.

Want to hear the other good bits? Some rather brainy folk have worked on this book to make sure it's fun and informative. So what are you waiting for? Peel back the pages and be amazed at Kent's very own story.

Timeline showing which period (dates and people) each spread is talking about

'Spot this!' game with hints at something to find in Kent

THE FACTS

An imaginary account of what it was like for children growing up in Kent

THE EVIDENCE

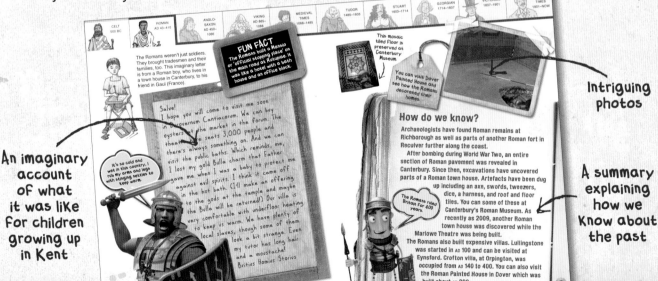

Intriguing photos

A summary explaining how we know about the past

Fun Facts to amaze you!

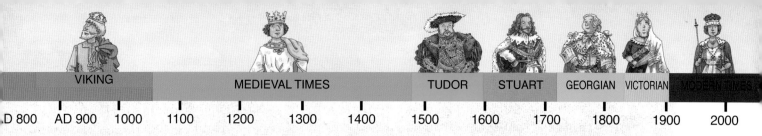

Contents

CELT 500 BC	ROMAN AD 43–410	ANGLO-SAXON AD 450–1066	VIKING AD 865–1066	MEDIEV TIMES 1066–14

Roman Invasion

It's May AD 43 and Emperor Claudius has chosen Aulus Plautius, one of his best generals, to lead the invasion of Britain! After a rough sea crossing from Gaul (France), 50,000 Roman soldiers land on the Kent coast. The Britons have traded with the Romans for years, but this time, the Romans are here to stay.

Gateway to Briton

The Romans first tried to invade Britain in 55 BC, but didn't make it across the Channel because of a storm. But they traded with the Britons. The Romans named the Kent area 'Cantium' after the people who lived there, the Cantiaci Celts.

When Aulus Plautius landed on the Kent coast, he divided his men into three divisions ready to fight the Britons. But the Celtic royal households had been having trouble keeping control amongst their people. So they were glad when the Romans arrived. They realised that linking up with the Romans would help them keep law and order. So with no resistance, the Roman soldiers made their way across the Wantsum Channel to set up camp at Rutupiae, now known as Richborough.

The Romans wasted no time in establishing Richborough as a military and naval base. Storehouses and granaries were built as well as shops, houses, army barracks, temples, roads and an amphitheatre. Soon, lots of Britons came to live and work near the fort because there was so much going on there.

The lighthouse at Dover Castle was built by the Romans as a beacon for shipping.

4

...AD 43 ROMANS INVADE BRITAIN...AD 130 DOVER LIGHTHOUSE BUILT...

Who were the Romans?

The Romans came from Italy and had built up a huge empire covering most of Europe. The new Roman emperor, Claudius, wanted to show he was a bold and warlike leader. He also wanted Britain's riches, such as grain, tin, iron and gold.

The powerful Roman army landed in south-east England. They quickly built forts at Rutupiae (Richborough) and Regulbium (Reculver). Towns grew up around Roman temples at Durovernum Cantiacorum (Canterbury) and Durobrivae (Rochester). The Romans paved the ancient track called Watling Street so that soldiers could move quickly between the ports at Dubris (Dover) and Londinium (London). Magnificent villas were constructed at Lullingstone, Crofton and Dover. Canterbury soon became the capital of Cantium as the roads from Dover, Richborough, Reculver and Lympne all met up there.

SPOT THIS!

Spot the ruins of a triumphal arch built by the Romans at Richborough to celebrate their invasion.

The Empire Ends

By about AD100, the Romans ruled most of the south and west of Britain. But they didn't succeed in conquering the far north of England, or Scotland or Wales. Nor did they invade Ireland.

During the third century, the Roman Empire was being attacked from all sides. The Saxons from Germany raided the Kent coast. Forts at Reculver, Richborough, Dover and Lympne formed part of a chain of defences that became known as the Saxon Shore.

Roman troops finally left Britain to defend their homeland in AD 410.

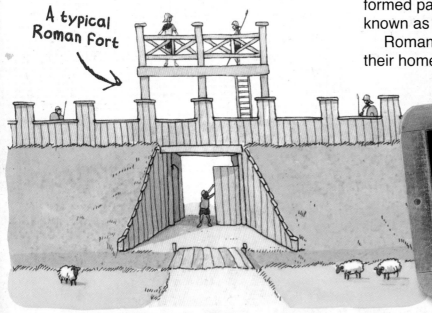

A typical Roman fort

FUN FACT
Roman Emperor, Julius Caesar, wrote of the Britons that "of all these tribes, by far the most civilised are they who dwell in Cantium".

The Romans weren't just soldiers. They brought tradesmen and their families, too. This imaginary letter is from a Roman boy, who lives in a town house in Canterbury, to his friend in Gaul (France).

FUN FACT
The Romans built a Mansio or 'official stopping place' on the main road at Rutupiae. It was like a hotel with a bath house and an office block.

It's so cold and wet in this country, I rub my arms and legs with stinging nettles to keep warm.

Salve!

I hope you will come to visit me soon in Durovernum Cantiacorum. We can buy oysters at the market in the forum. The theatre here seats 3,000 people and there's always something on. And we can visit the public baths. Which reminds me, I lost my gold Bulla charm that Father gave me when I was a baby to protect me against evil spirits. I think it came off in the hot bath. (I'll make an offering to the gods at the temple and maybe the Bulla will be returned!) Our villa is very comfortable with underfloor heating to keep us warm. We have plenty of local slaves, though some of them look a bit strange. Even my tutor has long hair and a moustache!

Britius Homius Storius

This mosaic tiled floor is preserved at Canterbury Museum.

You can visit Dover Painted House and see how the Romans decorated their homes.

How do we know?

Archaeologists have found Roman remains at Richborough as well as parts of another Roman fort in Reculver, further along the coast.

After bombing during World War Two, an entire section of Roman pavement was revealed in Canterbury. Since then, excavations have uncovered parts of a Roman town house. Artefacts have been dug up including an axe, swords, tweezers, dice, a harness, and roof and floor tiles. You can see some of these at Canterbury's Roman Museum. As recently as 2009, another Roman town house was discovered while the Marlowe Theatre was being built.

The Romans also built expensive villas. Lullingstone was started in AD 100 and can be visited at Eynsford. Crofton Villa, at Orpington, was occupied from AD 140 to 400. You can also visit the Roman Painted House in Dover which was built about AD 200.

The Romans ruled Britain for 400 years.

Raiders!

Since the Romans left, Angles and Saxons from Germany have been attacking all along the south-east coast. The raiders steal everything that is worth having and then go home. But, this time, they have brought women and children with them. They plan to settle here. The local people of Cantware (Kent) will have to learn to live alongside their new neighbours.

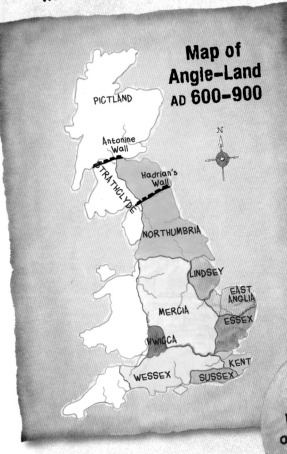

Map of Angle-Land AD 600-900

PICTLAND

Antonine Wall

STRATHCLYDE

Hadrian's Wall

NORTHUMBRIA

LINDSEY

EAST ANGLIA

MERCIA

ESSEX

HWICCA

KENT

WESSEX   SUSSEX

Kent was known as the Kingdom of Cantware.

Who were the Anglo-Saxons?

The Anglo-Saxons were not a single tribe, but a mixture of different peoples from the areas of Europe we now know as Denmark and Germany. Among these were the Angles, the Saxons and the Jutes. All of them had fast-growing populations, and were eager to find new land to settle on.

Saxon raiders began attacking the south-east coast of Britain in about AD 350. After Roman power collapsed in around AD 410, other Anglo-Saxon groups crossed the sea to southern Britain. Within two centuries, they had taken control of all the land up to the borders of Scotland and Wales. It became known as 'Angle-land', or England.

Almost all Anglo-Saxons were farmers. In Kent, they became experts at growing cereal crops and fruit in the rich soil. They also grazed sheep on the marshes around the coast.

Cantware

In AD 449, High King Vortigern, a leading ruler of the Britons, asked two Jutes from Germany to help him protect Cantware from invaders. Bede later recorded in his *History of England*, that Hengist and his brother Horsa arrived at Ebbsfleet in around AD 450. They were so good at keeping the place safe that Vortigern rewarded them with land on the Isle of Thanet.

Hengist and Horsa soon realized how weak the British defences were and began to take over the kingdom of Cantware. They fought Vortigern in AD 455 at the bloody Battle of Aylesford. Although Horsa was killed, Hengist won. Hengist now asked the Saxons to help him secure his power.

Cantware continued to be ruled by Anglo-Saxon kings until Vikings from the north of Europe began raiding the coast. By AD 865 the people of Kent were paying the Vikings to live peacefully with them.

Angles and Saxons together are called the Anglo-Saxons.

FUN FACT
The Saxon Shore Way is a 260-kilometre coastal walk along the Roman and Saxon fortifications that defended the Kent coast.

SPOT THIS!

Can you spot Reculver Towers which stand on the site of St Mary's Saxon church?

Most Saxons lived in huts like this.

A Holy Place

The Anglo-Saxons brought with them their own Germanic languages. These gradually mixed with the Roman and Celtic speech of the locals, and developed into the English language we use today. Many common English words, such as 'hundred', 'ghost', 'night' and 'horse', were originally Anglo-Saxon words.

The Anglo-Saxons also encouraged Christianity among the Britons, who had been pagans worshipping many different nature gods. In AD 597 Saint Augustine, who was sent by the Pope in Rome, soon converted many Britons to Christianity. He set up a monastery at Canterbury which became known as St Augustine's Abbey.

Queen Bertha was the wife of Ethelbert, King of Kent in AD 596. She was a Christian but her husband was a pagan. This is an imaginary account from a servant in Queen Bertha's household.

There's a statue of Queen Bertha outside the Abbey.

AD 597

The king has become a Christian! My lady, Queen Bertha, is already a Christian of course. The king restored one of the churches the Romans left behind and dedicated it to St Martin of Tours.

But Bishop Augustine landed on the Isle of Thanet with some Benedictine monks. The King welcomed Augustine and his friends and gave him St Martin's church. People like Augustine and listen to him. Now it's the end of the year, and the King has converted to Christianity like many others in Kent. I'm going to do it next week.

Now Augustine is planning to build our first cathedral within the Roman city walls of Canterbury. He is also founding a monastery of St Peter and St Paul outside the walls. After years of being in ruins, Canterbury is a very busy place again, full of visitors!

Canterbury Cathedral has been rebuilt several times.

FUN FACT
St Augustine was the first Archbishop of Canterbury. There have now been 105 Archbishops!

The Latin word for a seat is 'cathedra' from which the word cathedral comes.

St Augustine's Abbey was built near the burial place of Anglo-Saxon Kings and Queens.

Monasteries grew rich and powerful in Saxon times.

How do we know?

St Martin's Church, where Queen Bertha and King Ethelbert worshipped with Augustine still stands in Canterbury. It is the oldest church in the English-speaking world and holds regular services.

After King Henry VIII destroyed St Augustine's Abbey in 1538, it was left to fall into ruins and had almost been forgotten. Now there is a museum full of items found at the site. You can also walk around the remains and foundations of the abbey and see the changes that were made over its 1000-year history.

CELT
500 BC

ROMAN
AD 43–410

ANGLO-
SAXON
AD 450–
1066

VIKING
AD 865–
1066

MEDIE
TIME
1066–1

Invicta!

It is 1066. William, Duke of Normandy, has landed on the beach in Pevensey, Sussex. During a ferocious battle at Hastings, the English king, Harold, is killed along with most of his soldiers. William marches his men to Dover. At the site of the old Roman lighthouse, they build an earthwork castle with a wooden keep and fortifications.

I am one of William the Conqueror's men. William conquered all of England!

Normans

William claimed that an old English King, Edward, had promised him the English throne. King Harold was fighting other invaders in the north of England when William invaded. Harold marched his army south to fight William. The tired English army were easily defeated. William, now the Conqueror, crowned himself William I.

William marched through Kent towards London. Local tradition tells how the people of Kent fought them off. Proud that they were not conquered or defeated, they adopted the name 'Invicta', which means unconquered. Invicta is still the county motto today.

William and the Normans soon took control of England. They also conquered parts of Ireland and, later, Wales. They established a strong government. Only Scotland remained independent.

Dover Castle stands guard over the shortest sea crossing between France and Britain.

Priests and Pilgrims

In 1154, a new Plantagenet king, Henry II, was crowned. Henry made Thomas Becket Archbishop of Canterbury in 1162. But Becket upheld the power of the Pope and the Church in Rome against Henry's wishes. Henry is reported to have been furious with Becket.

On 29 December 1170, Thomas Becket was praying in Canterbury Cathedral when four of Henry's knights burst in. They demanded that Becket apologise to the King but he refused. The knights stabbed the Archbishop with such violence that the last blow broke the tip of the sword.

Becket was declared a martyr and a saint and soon pilgrims flocked to Canterbury. Henry was very powerful and rebuilt Dover castle to impress would-be invaders from France, Scotland and Flanders.

SPOT THIS!

Can you spot the memorial at Canterbury Cathedral where Thomas Becket was killed?

FUN FACT

'Cinq' is French for 'five'. The Normans spoke French and French was spoken at the royal court until Tudor times.

People enjoyed throwing rotten food at criminals locked in the local pillory.

I only smuggled wool across the English Channel!

Cinque Ports

The Cinque (said like Sink) Ports Confederation began around this time when five ports at Hastings, Romney, Hythe, Dover and Sandwich were granted a royal charter. The towns were expected to provide ships and men to defend the coast against attack and to protect trade across the English Channel. In return, the ports received many privileges. The Cinque Ports were part of England's defences during the Hundred Years War with France between 1337 and 1453.

In 1348 a deadly disease, the Black Death, arrived from Europe. It swept through the Cinque Ports, and the rest of the country, killing more than a third of the population.

CELT
500 BC

ROMAN
AD 43–410

ANGLO-SAXON
AD 450–1066

VIKING
AD 865–1066

MEDIE
TIME
1066–

Forts and Ships

Henry VIII has broken England's links with the Roman Catholic Church in Rome. He has destroyed England's abbeys, including St Augustine's, and has taken their treasures to pay for new forts and ships. Now Henry is building coastal forts against a possible invasion by the Catholic armies of France and Spain. On the Medway, the shipbuilders are busy constructing warships.

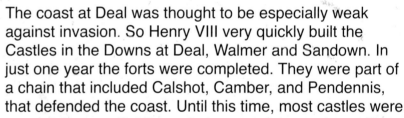

Castle Chain

A Tudor warship

The coast at Deal was thought to be especially weak against invasion. So Henry VIII very quickly built the Castles in the Downs at Deal, Walmer and Sandown. In just one year the forts were completed. They were part of a chain that included Calshot, Camber, and Pendennis, that defended the coast. Until this time, most castles were also homes. But these forts were only used as military posts. Inside, the rooms were very basic. Instead of tall castle walls they had lower, strong stone walls and all the towers of the forts faced the sea. The Tudors developed better guns so the forts were designed with platforms used as gun ports. The squat, rounded turrets were also used to deflect incoming cannon balls.

Henry also built special military ships with gun ports. During the winter months, these ships were moored on the Medway. These ships were the beginning of the English navy.

...1485 HENRY VII BECOMES FIRST TUDOR KING...1554 WYATT REBELLION...

The Tudors

In 1485, the nobles of Lancaster won the Battle of Bosworth, ending the Wars of the Roses. The victory brought a new family to the throne of England – the Tudors.

The Tudor monarchs were strong and ruthless rulers. Henry VIII, who became king in 1509, took away powers from his nobles so that he and his Parliament had more control.

When Mary I became Queen in 1553 she wanted to marry the Catholic King Philip of Spain. Sir Thomas Wyatt took men from Kent to London in 1554 to protest. It was known as Wyatt's Rebellion. The rebels were imprisoned or executed and Wyatt was hanged, drawn and quartered.

When Mary died in 1558, her half-sister Elizabeth I became Queen. She established a royal dockyard in Chatham that was used for over 400 years.

Some say that Drake was no better than a pirate!

FUN FACT
The King's School, Canterbury, might be the oldest school in England. Started by St Augustine in AD 597, it was given a Royal Charter in 1541.

SPOT THIS!
Deal Castle, built in 1540, has 119 gun positions. Can you see the shape of the Tudor Rose?

Peace and Poetry

The Tudor Age was a dazzling time for Britain. There was a long period of peace which helped the country to become richer. Sailors, such as Sir Francis Drake, opened up new trading routes and founded colonies overseas.

In Kent, the population grew. Flemish weavers had settled in Kent in the 1300s. They created some of the finest cloth in Europe which later brought great wealth to Tenterden, Biddenden, Cranbrook and Staplehurst. Henry VIII loved the cherries that the weavers brought with them from Flanders. So he got his head gardener to grow cherries in Kent. Soon the county had flourishing cherry orchards growing alongside the hop gardens.

The sixteenth century also produced some of Britain's greatest artists, composers and writers. Christopher Marlowe was born in Canterbury in 1564 and went to the King's School. He wrote plays that are still popular today. He was mysteriously stabbed to death in Deptford in 1593.

CELT
500 BC

ROMAN
AD 43–410

ANGLO-
SAXON
AD 450–
1066

VIKING
AD 865–
1066

MEDIE
TIMI
1066–

Henry VIII's second wife, Anne Boleyn, lived at Hever Castle when she was a child and she returned in 1528, before she was married, to stay with her family. In this imaginary account, a page called Will tells us why.

Phew! This candle's hot...oh no, I hope I haven't caught the English Sweate!

June 1528

The Boleyn family have come back to Hever. My master, Thomas Boleyn, is an important man in King Henry's court. But everyone has left the court, because a terrible illness called the English Sweate is spreading. It's what killed Prince Arthur, the king's older brother!

But the Sweate is now here too. Anne, my master's youngest daughter is ill. She complains of shivers and headaches and terrible pains in her legs. She is so ill that the King has sent his own doctor to care for her. And the King is coming to visit her in the hope that she will recover.

FUN FACT
No one ever found out what caused the English Sweate or made it spread. Mostly rich people caught it and some died within hours of becoming ill.

Henry VIII gave Hever Castle to his fourth wife, Anne of Cleves.

Henry VIII made himself head of the church in England.

Anne Boleyn was Elizabeth I's mother.

How do we know?

Some of the Boleyn family's possessions are still at Hever Castle. Two of Anne's prayer books are also kept there. You can see her signature in the books. When Henry VIII came to visit, he brought private locks to put on all the doors wherever he visited. His servants must have forgotten one of the locks when Henry visited Hever because it is still there today.

You can explore the ruins of St Augustine's Abbey as Henry VIII's soldiers left it. Many paintings survive to show us what the Tudor kings and queens looked like and how they dressed. Ballads, such as Greensleeves, and plays from William Shakespeare and Christopher Marlowe, tell some of their stories too.

Henry VIII had six wives: Catherine, Anne, Jane, Anne, Kathryn and Katherine.

Chalybeate and Change

In 1606 a young nobleman, Dudley Lord North, discovered that drinking from the 'chalybeate spring' in Tunbridge Wells made him feel better. Word spread and by Georgian times, visitors flocked to the town to drink from the iron-rich water. Amongst other things, the Georgians thought the water would cure 'a moist brain'. It soon became the playground of the nobility and royalty. They came to 'take the waters', but also to enjoy the dancing and gambling.

The Georges

George III reigned from 1760 until 1820.

Tunbridge Wells was a favourite place of Queen Anne's, until her infant son fell on the clay pantiles. She gave the town £100 to replace the pantiles with flagstones, but the name stuck. When Queen Anne, the last of the Stuart monarchs, died in 1714 she had no surviving children. The British crown passed to her German cousin, George I who came from Hanover. He did not speak any English, so left the daily running of affairs to his council, which was led by Robert Walpole. Walpole became Britain's first prime minister.

George I was followed onto the throne by three other King Georges, who reigned until 1830. This period is known as the Georgian age. But by late Georgian times, the royal family had become very unpopular. People thought they were weak and corrupt.

SPOT THIS!

Can you spot the chalybeate spring in the Pantiles at Tunbridge Wells?

...1714 GEORGE I BECOMES KING...1808 MARTELLO TOWERS BUILT...

Two Revolutions

Britain saw huge changes during the Georgian era, largely thanks to what we call the Industrial Revolution. Farming, mining and manufacturing were transformed by the invention of steam powered machines. New canals and roads were built. Britain became the biggest producer of goods in the world – and the richest.

But another revolution led Britain into a major war. The French Revolution of 1789 saw France build a strong army and conquer several countries in Europe. The French leader, Napoleon, even had plans to invade Britain. He saw England as the key to conquering the rest of Europe and amassed 130,000 troops and 2000 boats on the French coast at Boulogne.

A Martello tower at Folkestone.

The rich became richer and the poor became poorer in Georgian times.

FUN FACT
Gangs of smugglers took wool into France and brought tea back to Kent to avoid taxes.

New Defences

Between 1804 and 1808, more defensive towers were built to add to the Tudor coastal forts. Known as Martello Towers, they were 12 metres high and held a garrison of one officer and up to 25 soldiers. William Pitt, the Prime Minister, was persuaded to build a 45-kilometre-long canal as another military defence. Work started on the Royal Military Canal on 30 October 1804. Set in from the coast, it was hoped that the canal would take any French invaders by surprise. It would also mean that smugglers could be spotted by the soldiers that manned the canal.

The Dutch, British, Belgians and Germans grouped their armies together. Under the leadership of the British Duke of Wellington, they fought Napoleon and his army at Waterloo in Belgium. On 18 June 1815, the Battle of Waterloo left Napoleon defeated and Wellington became a hero.

Mr Pitt, the prime minister, and the Duke of York were keen to construct the Royal Military Canal on Romney Marsh. The landowners of Romney Marsh were persuaded to give up their land for it to be built. This imaginary account is written by Tom, a farmer's son.

Digging this canal is thirsty work. This Faversham ale is just the job!

April 1809

At last the canal is finished! Pa can't believe how long it's taken them – four and a half years! He says his Romney sheep could have been grazing the land all that time. But he had to give up the land for the canal to run through it. Some of Pa's farm workers left to work on the canal. Sometimes there were as many as 1500 local men digging the trenches. Now it runs from Seaford until it meets the River Rother near Rye. Some people think it's been a waste of time because Napoleon isn't interested in invading Britain any more. All that work for nothing! And it cost £234,310*. People on the Marsh are calling it 'Mr Pitt's Ditch'!

(*That's about £8 million today!)

A shepherd hut was moved to new pasture with the flock.

FUN FACT

Soldiers boots were made of fabric. But Wellington didn't like getting his feet wet so he got his boots made of leather and started a trend!

The arms of the Lord Warden of the Cinque Port.

How do we know?

Since 1708, Walmer Castle, on the Kent coast, has been the official home of the Lord Warden of the Cinque Ports. Over the years the Cinque Ports Confederation grew to include Rye, Winchelsea, Deal and Ramsgate, Faversham, Folkestone, Margate, Lydd and Tenterden. Two of the most famous Lord Wardens were William Pitt and the Duke of Wellington. Both of them had been Prime Ministers. Walmer Castle has museums dedicated to both men and they have lots of their personal possessions in them. In the Wellington Museum you can see an original pair of Wellington boots and the Duke's Lord Warden uniform. The Pitt Museum is in Pitt's study and has a chair that he sat in to read books.

Britain built an empire in North America, India, Africa and Australia.

21

Steaming Ahead

The first steam public railway opened in 1825 and rail tracks have been spreading across the UK ever since. The South Eastern Railway opens in Kent in 1836 and is the main route from Dover to London. Branch lines are added to link up with Tunbridge Wells, Maidstone and Canterbury as well as other parts of Kent.

The population of Kent more than doubled in Queen Victoria's reign.

FUN FACT

Dickens retrieved the unfinished manuscript of 'Our Mutual Friend' from a rail accident you can read about opposite.

British Empire

In 1837, Victoria became Queen, aged only 18 years old. She reigned for over 60 years, until 1901. During her reign, the British Empire grew to cover nearly a quarter of the globe, and included many millions of people. The Empire gave Britain vast supplies of valuable raw materials. It was also a huge market for selling goods manufactured at home. Troops were stationed in most parts of the Empire, giving Britain a lot of power in the world.

The spread of the railways meant that goods from Kent could be transported quickly. People from the countryside flocked to the towns to take jobs in the expanding ports, mills and factories. Paper mills were built near the Rivers Darent, Medway and Stour. The chalk and clay in Kent was perfect for making cement and bricks. In Cliffe, near Rochester, a cement works was opened in 1854. Brickworks were opened in Sittingbourne and Pluckley.

Work and play

Working hours were long and wages low. Young children often had to work as well as their parents. Living conditions were poor. In the over-crowded cities there was poor sanitation and little fresh water. Diseases like cholera spread fast and many people died.

During Queen Victoria's reign, new laws reduced the number of hours women and children could work. Inspectors were appointed to check the safety standards of factories and mines. Wages were increased, and, in 1871, the first Monday Bank Holidays were introduced. It gave people in London the chance to travel by train to seaside towns such as Broadstairs, Hythe and Margate. Now that everyone had some free time, sport was no longer only for the rich. Football and cricket teams began to play regular fixtures.

SPOT THIS!

Dickens' story, Bleak House, was based on the house in Broadstairs where his family spent summer holidays.

Hop pickers came from all over Kent and from London for the harvest.

THE DAILY NEWS
9th June, 1865 • Your favourite local newspaper

FAMOUS AUTHOR IN RAIL CRASH

Novelist Charles Dickens, who lives in Gad's Hill near Rochester, was returning with friends from a trip to France when the train in which they were travelling came off the tracks at Staplehurst, Kent. The Folkestone Boat Express was on a cast iron bridge that was undergoing repair. It is believed that the rail engineers were not expecting the train to pass. All but one of the carriages fell into the River Beult below the bridge. Charles Dickens and his companions were in the First Class Carriage, which remained on the track. Eyewitnesses report that Mr Dickens behaved heroically, leading all the passengers in his own carriage to safety. He then went to the assistance of those in other carriages and to tend to the injured. Ten people died and 49 were injured in the incident.

Wartime

It's 1938 and war is threatening to overtake Europe and the rest of the world. At Dover Castle, secret plans are being carried out to turn this twelfth-century coastal fortress into an operations headquarters. By the start of World War Two, the Castle will be a bomb-proof barracks for the fortress commander, coastal and anti-aircraft gun operations, and the Royal Navy's Dover headquarters.

Keep calm and carry on!

Two World Wars

When Queen Victoria died in 1901, Britain was one of the world's richest and most powerful nations, with a massive empire and strong armed forces. But soon the British were plunged into long and costly world wars. In World War One, over a million men were killed.

World War Two killed a vast number of civilians as well as soldiers. Enemy bombs destroyed large areas of major towns. The expense of the fighting also left Britain with huge debts. The British Empire began to shrink, as many countries demanded their freedom.

Government Air Raid Warning in 1939:

When you hear the warning take cover at once. Remember that most of the injuries in an air raid are caused not by direct hits by bombs but by flying fragments of debris or by bits of shells.

TUDOR
1485–1603

STUART
1603–1714

GEORGIAN
1714–1837

VICTORIAN
1837–1901

MODERN
TIMES
1901–NOW

Secret Tunnels

By the end of May 1940, Germany had captured France. With another threat of invasion from the German army, Dover Castle was called upon again to defend the country. A complex series of tunnels had been dug during the Napoleonic Wars. Now these became air raid shelters and as many as 10,500 troops were housed to fight the enemy.

Meanwhile, British and French troops were trapped on the beach at Dunkirk with the German army advancing. Vice-Admiral Betram Ramsay was the naval commander at Dover in charge of Operation Dynamo. This was a plan to evacuate troops from Dunkirk. In the space of 10 days, 338,000 troops were rescued on a fleet of passenger, cargo and 'little' ships from the beaches of Dunkirk.

SPOT THIS!

Spot this statue of Vice-Admiral Ramsay overlooking the harbour at Dover Castle.

Gateway to Britain

Britain took a long time to recover from the effects of World War Two. Fewer ships were built at Chatham Dockyard and less coal was needed from the Kent coal mines. But by the 1960s, the economy had grown strong again. Cheap fuel was needed, so a nuclear power station was opened at Dungeness. In 1973, Britain joined the Common Market, an organization which aimed to bring the countries of Europe closer together. In 1994 the Channel Tunnel was completed, linking Britain with mainland Europe. With the need for clean electricity, the world's largest offshore wind farm opened off the coast of Thanet in 2010.

Now citizens from all over Europe cross the Channel to work in Britain. Cargo ships and lorries transport freight to Britain from across the world. There are large container ports at Thamesport on the Isle of Grain and Ramsgate. Cruise ships take passengers on holiday from Dover.

FUN FACT
On 6th June, 1944 a dummy invasion was launched from Dover to fool the German army, while the real D-Day attack got underway in Normandy.

...1964 DUNGENESS NUCLEAR POWER STATION BUILT...1994 CHANNEL TUNNEL OPENS...

25

When war broke out in 1939, about 800,000 children were evacuated from towns and cities. It was hoped they would be safer from bombing in the countryside. But by 1940, the countryside around the Kent coast was so close to occupied France that it was known as Hellfire Corner. This imaginary story is told by Bobby who lives in a village not far from Folkestone. He is talking about the Prime Minister, Mr Churchill.

You can see a replica Hurricane and Spitfire at the Battle of Britain Memorial!

18th July 1940

Mr Churchill said on the radio, "The Battle of Britain is about to begin." We didn't realize it would be happening over Kent! There's an RAF station not far from here. We've seen lots of Hurricanes and Spitfires overhead during the day. We see German Heinkels and Messerschmitts too. One minute it's quiet then, suddenly, you hear a roar of engines and the rat-tat-tat as they fire at each other. They're so close you can almost see their faces! Then there's flames and thick, black smoke as the planes plummet like giant fireworks from the sky. Sometimes, pilots bail out and their parachutes billow up into the clouds. They drop like stones into the fields. When my mum isn't looking, I sneak over to check out the wreckage. I've managed to find a bit of a propeller and some buttons from a uniform. I even found a bullet clip from a German plane! Lots of my friends have been evacuated from Kent. Their mums think it's too dangerous to live here. But my mum says we have to stay to help my dad and grandad run our farm. She says growing fruit and potatoes is our part of the war effort. We're digging for victory!

The Battle of Britain Memorial at Capel-le-Ferne lists the names of almost 3000 who took part.

TUDOR
1485–1603

STUART
1603–1714

GEORGIAN
1714–1837

VICTORIAN
1837–1901

MODERN
TIMES
1901–NOW

FUN FACT
In 1943 bouncing bombs were tested near Reculver. RAF 617 Squadron used them in the famous Dambuster Raids to burst German dams.

Everyone carried gas masks during wartime in case of a gas attack. But they were never needed.

How do we know?

The Battle of Britain Museum near Folkestone is exactly where RAF Station Hawkinge was during the Second World War. The airfield was only ten minutes flying time from the Luftwaffe (German air force) fighter airfields in Pas-de-Calais. Now, you can see the relics of over 600 crashed aircraft from the War and some original aircraft hangars and 1940s buildings.

In Ramsgate there is another museum at the old RAF Station Manston. There you can still see the remains of the longest and widest runway in southern Britain. It was built to allow a safe haven to badly damaged aircraft returning from Europe. Photographs from the time and newsreel films shown in cinemas give us an idea of what life was like in wartime.

It took years to rebuild the towns after the bombing of World War Two.

CELT 500 BC	ROMAN AD 43–410	ANGLO-SAXON AD 450–1066	VIKING AD 865–1066	MEDIE TIME 1066–

Today and Tomorrow

Kent is known as the Garden of England because, for many centuries, it was famous for growing hops, for beer, and apples. Today, there are only a few hop gardens left but the county is still famous for growing fruit. There are also vineyards in Kent, producing wine in the county for the first time since the Normans!

⬆ Traditional Kent crafts and farm breeds, such as this Romney sheep, are on display at the Kent County Show, held every year at Detling.

You can feel proud to be from Kent!

⬆ Invicta, the flag of Kent, shows a white horse on a red background. The white horse has been linked with the emblem of Horsa the Jute.

⬅ The Turner Contemporary gallery in Margate combines old and new. The original harbour building, Droit House, stands beside a modern gallery showing work by local artists such as Tracey Emin.

FUN FACT

The Channel Tunnel is the longest undersea tunnel in the world. It is 50.5 kilometres in total with 38 kilometres of it under the English Channel.

⬆ Once a home for nobility and kings, today Leeds Castle is open to the public.

⬆ Oast houses make up part of Kent Life, near Maidstone, which celebrates the history of Kent's countryside and farming life.

⬅ Old windmills, like this one at Woodchurch, still survive. Will the new wind farms last as long?

⬅ The Marlowe Theatre in Canterbury is named after Christopher Marlowe, the famous playwright.

How will they know?

How will future generations know what Kent was like for us, now? The internet is a great way of recording the present. Hundreds of years from now someone may be looking at your photo or reading your blog. You're making history!

Glossary

Abbey – a building where monks or nuns live and work. An Abbot is in charge of monks, an Abbess is in charge of nuns.

AD – a short way to write 'anno Domini', which is Latin and means 'in the year of Our Lord', i.e. after the birth of Christ.

Air raid – during World War Two, enemy planes dropped bombs on Britain. This was an air raid. Sirens sounded to warn people that planes were coming, and everyone hid in air raid shelters.

Amphitheatre – a round open-air theatre surrounded by seats which rise from a central arena so everyone can see and hear.

Archaeologist – a person who studies the past by examining buildings and objects left behind by previous people and cultures.

Artefact – another word for an object, often an archaeological one.

Ballad – a song written as a poem that tells a story.

Barracks – a building where soldiers stay.

BC – these initials mean 'Before Christ' and are used to indicate the period of time before Jesus Christ was born.

Benedictine – a monk or nun who joins the Christian religious community that follows the teachings of St Benedict.

Black Death, the – another name for the Plague.

Charter – written permission to do something. It is often a Royal Charter, meaning the king or queen has given permission.

Cholera – a deadly disease caused by filthy water.

Christian – anyone who believes Christ is the son of God and follows his teachings.

Dockyard – an area beside the water where boats and ships can be built and repaired.

Evacuate – leave your home and live somewhere else for safety.

Fort or fortress – a large, strong building offering military support and protection.

Forum – a meeting or place where people discuss things.

Garrison – where soldiers stay while they are guarding a place.

Gas mask – used in World War Two, this mask protected you from breathing poisonous gas.

Keep – the main tower within the walls of a castle or fortress.

Martyr – someone prepared to die for their beliefs, usually their religion.

Monastery – a place where monks live and worship.

Monk – a male member of a religious community that has rules of poverty, chastity and obedience.

Mosaic – small pieces of coloured glass or stone stuck together to form a design.

Oast house – a cone shaped building used for drying hops.

Pagan – someone who believes in more than one god.

Pope – the official name for the man who heads the Roman Catholic Church.

Relic – an object (or custom) that has survived from the past.

Roman Catholic – a member of the Christian religion which considers the Pope to be the head of its church.

Weaver – someone who uses a machine called a loom to weave threads together to make cloth.

Index

Acknowledgements

The publishers would like to thank the following people and organizations
for their permission to reproduce material on the following pages:

Front Cover: Alison Hancock/Shutterstock, syringa/Shutterstock; back cover: Route66/Shutterstock, mirrormere/Shutterstock; p4: Deborah McCague/Shutterstock; p5: Midnightblueowl/Wikipedia; p 7: Linda Spashett (Storyebook)/Wikipedia © Canterbury Museums and Galleries, The Roman Painted House; p9: Alan Gordine/Shutterstock; p10: Laura Leahy; p11: Route66/Shutterstock; p12: Filip Fuxa/Shutterstock; p13: Laura Leahy; Lieven Smits/Wikipedia; p16: Ivanovskyy/Shutterstock; p18: Mike Bartlett/Tunbridge Wells Borough Council; p19: David Flowler/Shutterstock; p20: Kent Life; p21: Graham Padruig/Wikipedia; p23: David Burrow/Shutterstock, Museum of English Rural Life, University of Reading; p25: Barry Arnold/Flickr; p26: Battle of Britain Trust; p27: York Museums Trust; p28: gengirl/Shutterstock, Laura Leahy; p29: Dan Breckwoldt/Shutterstock, Kent Life, Laura Leahy, Rui Saraiva/Shutterstock.

All other images copyright of Hometown World

Written by Caroline Plaisted and Andrew Langley
Edited by Cathy Jones
Local history consultant: Dr Sheila Sweetinburgh
Designed by Sarah Allen

Illustrated by Kate Davies, Dynamo Ltd, Virginia Gray, Tim Hutchinson,
Peter Kent, Leighton Noyes, Nick Shewring and Tim Sutcliffe
Additional photographs by Alex Long

First published by HOMETOWN WORLD in 2013
Hometown World Ltd
7 Northumberland Buildings
Bath BA1 2JB

www.hometownworld.co.uk

Copyright © Hometown World Ltd 2013

ISBN 978-1-84993-245-5

CELT	ROMAN	ANGLO–SAXON	VIKING	MEDIEVAL TIMES
500 BC	AD 43–410	AD 450–1066	AD 865–1066	1066–1485